920
CON

Cone, Molly

The Ringling
brothers

C2

920
CON

Cone, Molly

The Ringling
brothers

C2

DATE	BORROWER'S NAME	
OCT 4 1973	Mark Gibson	
FEB 19 1975	Rickie G	
MAR 7		

The
Ringling
Brothers

By *Molly Cone* # THE RINGLING BROTHERS

Illustrated by James and Ruth McCrea

Thomas Y. Crowell Company • *New York*

CROWELL BIOGRAPHIES
Edited by Susan Bartlett Weber

LEONARD BERNSTEIN by Molly Cone
WILT CHAMBERLAIN by Kenneth Rudeen
CESAR CHAVEZ by Ruth Franchere
SAMUEL CLEMENS by Charles Michael Daugherty
CHARLES DREW by Roland Bertol
GORDON PARKS by Midge Turk
THE RINGLING BROTHERS by Molly Cone
JACKIE ROBINSON by Kenneth Rudeen
ELEANOR ROOSEVELT by Jane Goodsell
MARIA TALLCHIEF by Tobi Tobias
JIM THORPE by Thomas Fall
MALCOLM X by Arnold Adoff

COPYRIGHT © 1971 BY MOLLY CONE
ILLUSTRATIONS COPYRIGHT © 1971 BY JAMES AND RUTH MCCREA

MANUFACTURED IN THE UNITED STATES OF AMERICA

L. C. Card 70–132295

ISBN 0–690–70287–6
(Library edition 0–690–70288–4)

2   3   4   5   6   7   8   9   10

The
Ringling
Brothers

A CROWELL
BIOGRAPHY

DAN RIC[E]

Brilliant combination of Arenic
ATTRACTIONS

WEDNESDAY, MARCH 16th, 18[__]

A THOUSAND LAUGHS!

LARGEST & HEAVIEST ELEPHA[NT]
IN THE WORLD

TWO Performan[ces]
THIS DAY!

Come Boys and have some Fun!!

"THE CIRCUS IS COMING!" said the black and yellow circus bills to the people of McGregor. Elephants waved their trunks and clowns grinned from the sides of barns and fences.

The Ringling brothers woke up early in the morning on circus day. They ran down to the river to see the circus boat come in.

Al was the oldest. He was eighteen years old. Then came Gus, sixteen; Otto, twelve; Alfred Theodore, called Alf T., eight; Charlie, six; and John, who was only four. At home was Henry, the baby.

1

McGregor, Iowa, was a river town. The main street led to the Mississippi River. In 1870 boats steamed up and down with corn and cotton, wheat and lumber.

The younger Ringling boys often played on the river bank. They waved and shouted at the boats going by. They knew every boat by its whistle.

The circus boat came with blasts of whistles. It moved slowly up the river playing tunes from a calliope.

A calliope was a steam piano. The steam to make it play came from the same boiler that made the river boat go. The clanging melody brought everyone running.

The boys of McGregor crowded close to watch the boat unload. A few held their noses when the elephant came off. "Phew!" they said.

The Ringlings liked the way the elephant smelled. They liked the smell of the monkey, and the ponies, and the lion in the lion cage too.

They ran after the circus band and followed along behind it. They marched in time to the music of the circus parade. Together they crowded into the tent put up for the big circus show.

All of them held their breath as a man walked a rope stretched tight above their heads. They blinked as a juggler made plates spin. They gasped at the riders who stood on galloping horses. When the acrobat turned somersaults in the air, they whistled and clapped. They laughed at the clown who tried to do it too.

Ever after, the brothers called the circle in the center of the tent a "ring," just as the circus people did. The man with a whip who directed the horses was the "ringmaster." They called the tents "tops." The main circus tent was the "Big Top." A special show outside in a little top was a "side show."

For a long time after the circus had left McGregor, the sound of the wonderful calliope rang in their ears.

"What's the matter with them?" Papa Ringling wondered.

Mama Ringling rolled her eyes toward the ceiling as if it were easy to tell. "The circus is what is the matter with them," she said.

"Some day we're going to have a circus of our own," Al said. He stretched a rope over the hay in his father's barn. He began to practice tightrope walking.

They'd soon forget about the circus, their
father thought. They'd all be harness makers one
day, as he was. He let them ride his bony old
horse in the field behind the harness shop. They
took turns trying to ride standing up.

Their mother let them have the chipped plates
in her cupboard for juggling. She dyed their old
long underwear red for acrobatic tights.

Day after day they juggled plates and practiced
tumbling in the middle of the big kitchen.

Mama Ringling finally threw up her hands.
"What is this—a house or a circus tent!" she
complained.

They made a tent out of an old rag carpet and some horse blankets. A toy cart painted red became a circus wagon. The boys chased the town's stray goat until they caught it. They named the goat Billy Rainbow and tried to teach it tricks.

With the goat and wagon, the boys marched

down McGregor's main street in a circus parade.
Al blew a bugle. Otto beat a drum. The others
made as much noise as they could on a fife, a
jew's harp, and harmonicas.

"Come to the circus!" they hollered. "Come
to the circus!"

"It's something they'll grow out of," Mama Ringling said hopefully.

Papa Ringling was proud of his big American family. He had come from Germany to live in the United States when he was twenty-one. Mama's family had come from Alsace-Lorraine, which was part of France. One of the first things Papa Ringling did was change his last name to make it sound American. He became August *Ringling* instead of *Rüngeling*.

After the seven boys, a girl—Ida—was born. Eight children were a houseful, but Mama Ringling was a good cook and manager. Papa made the rules. Going to church on Sunday was one of them. No cheating—ever—was another one of his rules.

Papa Ringling was an expert harness maker. He had his own shop. But the Depression of 1873

brought hard times. He moved his large family
from McGregor to another little town close by,
and then to another. He worked for someone else
for a while, and then opened his own harness
shop again. Papa Ringling was a stubborn man.
He liked to be his own boss. Finally he moved his
business and his family to Baraboo, Wisconsin.

One by one, the Ringling brothers grew into
strong young men with cheerful round faces and
glossy black hair. But they didn't outgrow their
love for the circus.

Al went to work for a small traveling show.
He walked a tightrope and balanced a plow on his
head and juggled. When he came home to visit,
he brought Louise, the girl he had married.

Gus and Otto found jobs in harness shops in
nearby towns.

Alf T. and Charlie became their father's helpers at home in Baraboo. But neither liked the harness business. They spent their spare time practicing music together. Charlie played the violin and trombone. Alf T. blew a cornet. They played in an orchestra for town dances.

John didn't want to learn his father's business. He didn't want to go to school either. He ran away when he was twelve years old to start a business of his own. He had seen his mother add bluing to her washtub of clothes. John added some to scouring powder and began to sell this as a new cleaner for pots and pans. His father found him in the next town and brought him home.

But John ran away several more times. He didn't like school and didn't stay long enough to graduate.

Once his brothers locked him in his room with a French horn. They wouldn't let him out until he had learned to play it. John learned fast when he wanted to.

John was sixteen when Al came home to get his brothers together to start a Ringling show.

Otto, Alf T., Charlie, and John were all for it.

Henry was still too young to take part, and Gus decided to stay a harness maker.

The five brothers were the whole show themselves. Al's wife, Louise, and Mama Ringling made the costumes.

They gave their first show in 1882 in Mazo-manie, Wisconsin. Parading up the street, they played loud music to advertise their show. Otto pounded the drum. The others blew so hard on their instruments that their faces turned red. But not many people came to see them in the town hall that night.

The music they played to open the program came out a jangle. John's French horn squealed, Charlie's violin squeaked, Alf T.'s cornet blasted, and Al's horn screeched. When they bowed, Al bumped into Charlie and Charlie into Alf T. People began to laugh.

After that, though Al juggled hats and plates, Charlie played eight different instruments, and John told funny jokes, no one laughed or clapped very loud. Glumly the brothers packed up and moved on to the next town.

Alf T.

John

This time the music sounded better. The Ringlings went to one little town after another with their show. That winter they traveled all over Wisconsin, Iowa, North Dakota, and Minnesota.

They played in town halls, or old, empty stores. Once they gave a show in a hotel dining room after the dinner dishes had been cleared away. Sometimes they had to borrow chairs. Other times they made seats with empty boxes, or planks laid across sawhorses.

They traded tickets to their show for meals, or rooms to sleep in. Often they slept in waiting rooms of train stations. Sometimes it took all the money they earned just to pay for their train ride to the next town.

But they came back to Baraboo full of ideas. By the end of the next season they had saved enough to buy new band uniforms.

Now they played in high silk hats and long Prince Albert coats with brass buttons. The five brothers all started to grow bushy mustaches.

They began to plan for a show in a ring under a Big Top. They started with the help of a real circus clown. His name was Yankee Robinson. Yankee was an old man with white whiskers. He had worked in circuses for forty years and he knew all about the circus business. The Ringlings made him their partner.

They followed his advice and bought canvas
for one Big Top and one little top. They cut
down trees to make center poles for the two tops.
They built benches for seats under the Big Top.
They bought old farm wagons, painted and
decorated them, and hired big farm horses to pull
the wagons. For a side show, they got a farmer
who had taught his pig to do tricks. The pig was
their only trained animal.

The new Ringling Circus opened in Baraboo in May 1884. The brothers were still most of the show themselves. Each did two or three things—even Mrs. Al. She not only made the costumes, but she was the bareback rider too. In the band were a few more musicians. A hired acrobat and juggler were also part of the Big Top show.

The people of Baraboo filled every seat under the Big Top. They laughed at the clown and clapped loudly for every performer. Afterward they bought still more tickets to see the side show.

The Ringlings were excited by their success. After the show was over, they hurried to load

everything onto the wagons. Early in the morning, horses pulled them over the bumpy roads to the next town.

There the two tents were unpacked and set up,

and the show was given again. Then they were packed and moved on to another town.

When it rained, the roads turned to mud. It rained often in the early spring. That's why wagon shows were called "mud shows."

The Ringlings kept going all through the

spring and summer. Then they came back to Baraboo. They stowed everything in their father's barn for the winter. The brothers called Baraboo their "winter quarters."

There was plenty of work to do. The Big Top had to be mended during the winter. New acts had to be planned, new performers hired, and new costumes made.

Old Yankee Robinson died at the end of the first season, and from then on the five brothers were equal partners. Each was an equal manager too.

They talked over ideas and decided on everything together. They often argued loudly and bellowed at each other. But they usually gave a new idea a try even when they did not all agree.

Every one of their letters was signed "The Ringling Brothers"—no matter which brother wrote it. Even letters to their mother.

In those days, no one trusted circus people. Many traveling shows were full of thieves. They often stole the Monday wash right off the lines and took things out of houses while the people were watching the parade. Ticket sellers gave back less change than they should have when selling tickets. Some circus managers hired pickpockets to mix with the crowds.

The Ringlings did not cheat anyone. They did not hire anyone who cheated either.

Everyone working in their circus had to be polite as well as honest. They had to say "Yes Sir," and "No Sir," and give directions courteously. No one was allowed to talk back to customers.

This was a new kind of circus managing.

Other circus owners made fun of the Ringling rules. But the crowds that came grew larger.

The Ringlings' circus parade became longer.
Cages on wheels carried a hyena, a brown bear,
and a bald eagle. Soon there were more cages,
with elk, lions, monkeys, and a deer.

In 1888 the Ringlings proudly paraded with

their first elephants, named Babylon and Fannie.

The big elephants always walked from town to town behind the last wagon. They stamped on every bridge to be sure they could walk safely across it.

On the circus lot they helped move heavy loads. They raised the center poles for the tops with their trunks. In the ring, they were part of the show. They wore spangled robes on their backs, and kneeled down so that girls in tights could climb up to ride on their heads.

Babylon and Fannie cost a great deal of money. So did camels, lions, tigers, a zebra, and a giraffe. The Ringling brothers were almost always short of money. They kept adding more of everything to improve their circus.

Every year they made the Big Top bigger. They added dressing tops and wild-animal tops and food tops and many side-show tops. In some of the side shows were a fat lady, a living skeleton, a giant, a tattooed man, a snake charmer, a magician, a ventriloquist, and a dwarf.

31

All these people traveled with the circus. So did the animals and the cages and the animal trainers and the workers and the performers. Soon

wagons and horses couldn't carry them all. In 1890 the Ringling Circus began to go from town to town on the railroad.

Before long, Gus and Henry came to work in

their brothers' circus too. Now all seven brothers together ran the Ringling Circus. But Gus and Henry never became part of the partnership.

Soon all the Ringlings except Otto were married, and their wives often came along on the circus train too. So did Ida's sons, John and Henry North. The children grew up with the circus.

The five managers each had their own jobs to do. Al was the director of the circus show. Otto was the business manager. Alf T. planned the advertising. Charlie played in the band and looked after the circus people. John traveled to Europe to find new performers and new acts. Circus artists from all over the world came to perform under the Ringling Big Top.

Tumblers and acrobats made human ladders by standing on each other's shoulders. Equestrians jumped from the ring to the backs of galloping horses. Aerialists climbed ropes dangling from the tent ceiling to get to swings high above the center ring. Fliers somersaulted from trapezes. Acrobats walked or rode bicycles on a tightwire up in the air.

The audiences watched in amazement. They screamed when an acrobat fell into a net. Once John got so excited he swallowed his cigar.

Now the Ringlings' circus parade stretched for three miles. The band wagon filled the street from curb to curb. Forty elephants moved slowly along.

Blasting and screeching at the very end rolled
the Ringlings' steam calliope. The biggest, the
loudest calliope that ever was!

In 1902 the Ringling Brothers Circus was the second largest in the United States. The only bigger one was the Barnum and Bailey Circus.

A few years later, the Ringlings bought the Barnum and Bailey Circus. For a time they ran both separately. In 1918 they made the two big shows into one.

Every day fifteen hundred people and a thousand animals were moved from town to town in the Ringlings' circus train. It took hundreds of men and elephants to put up the Big Top. Under the Big Top were seats for twelve thousand people. In the center were three rings. Different acts went on in all three rings at one time.

The Ringling Bros. and Barnum and Bailey Combined Shows was the largest circus that ever moved across any country. It was the greatest show on earth.

It all seemed like magic to Mama and Papa Ringling. They saw five circus-struck boys turn into the most famous circus managers in the world.

John outlived all his brothers. For a long time he kept the Ringlings' circus going by himself. He built new winter quarters for the circus in Sarasota, Florida, and he built a house that was like a palace. Now John's house is a museum. He willed it to the State of Florida.

Today the Greatest Show on Earth has other owners. But no one who loves the circus will ever forget that it all was started by five brothers named Ringling.

ABOUT THE AUTHOR

Molly Cone has written many books of fiction for boys and girls of all ages. She is also the author of *The Jewish New Year*, *The Jewish Sabbath*, and *Purim*, in the Crowell Holiday Book series; *The Green, Green Sea* and *The House in the Tree*, in the Crowell Stories from Many Lands series; and *Leonard Bernstein*, in the Crowell Biography series.

Mrs. Cone, who was born in Tacoma, Washington, "grew up writing." After her student days at the University of Washington, she became an advertising copywriter. She did not write her first children's book, however, until she had three children of her own, when she discovered that the busier she was, the more time she had for writing.

Mrs. Cone lives in Seattle, Washington, with her husband and teen-age daughter. When at home, she swims, hikes, and enjoys spending winter weekends on the Washington or Oregon coast; when abroad, she "sightsees like crazy," whether in Mexico, in Israel, or in Greece and the other countries of Europe.

ABOUT THE ILLUSTRATORS

Both Ruth and James McCrea attended the Ringling School of Art in Sarasota, Florida. Here they were able to go behind the scenes at the circus' winter quarters—drawing the animals and talking with, watching, and drawing the performers. Here also, Mrs. McCrea several times rode atop an elephant in circus parades through the town of Sarasota. The McCreas have had sawdust in *their* shoes ever since.

They have a son and two daughters and now live in Bayport, New York.